WITHDRAWN

WITHDRAWN

WITHDRAWN

A Note from
Mary Pope Osborne About the

MAGIC TREE HOUSE®
FACT TRACKERS

When I write Magic Tree House® adventures, I love including facts about the times and places Jack and Annie visit. But when readers finish these adventures, I want them to learn even more. So that's why my husband, Will, and my sister, Natalie Pope Boyce, and I write a series of nonfiction books that are companions to the fiction titles in the Magic Tree House® series. We call these books Fact Trackers because we love to track the facts! Whether we're researching dinosaurs, pyramids, Pilgrims, sea monsters, or cobras, we're always amazed at how wondrous and surprising the real world is. We want you to experience the same wonder we do—so get out your pencils and notebooks and hit the trail with us. You can be a Magic Tree House® Fact Tracker, too!

Mary Pope Osborne

Here's what kids, parents, and teachers have to say about the Magic Tree House® Fact Trackers:

"They are so good. I can't wait for the next one. All I can say for now is prepare to be amazed!" —Alexander N.

"I have read every Magic Tree House book there is. The [Fact Trackers] are a thrilling way to get more information about the special events in the story." —John R.

"These are fascinating nonfiction books that enhance the magical time-traveling adventures of Jack and Annie. I love these books, especially *American Revolution*. I was learning so much, and I didn't even know it!" —Tori Beth S.

"[They] are an excellent 'behind-the-scenes' look at what the [Magic Tree House fiction] has started in your imagination! You can't buy one without the other; they are such a complement to one another." —Erika N., mom

"Magic Tree House [Fact Trackers] took my children on a journey from Frog Creek, Pennsylvania, to so many significant historical events! The detailed manuals are a remarkable addition to the classic fiction Magic Tree House books we adore!" —Jenny S., mom

"[They] are very useful tools in my classroom, as they allow for students to be part of the planning process. Together, we find facts in the [Fact Trackers] to extend the learning introduced in the fictional companions. Researching and planning classroom activities, such as our class Olympics based on facts found in *Ancient Greece and the Olympics*, help create a genuine love for learning!" —Paula H., teacher

Magic Tree House®
Fact Tracker

SHARKS AND OTHER PREDATORS

A nonfiction companion to
Magic Tree House® #53:
Shadow of the Shark

by Mary Pope Osborne
and Natalie Pope Boyce

illustrated by Carlo Molinari

A STEPPING STONE BOOK™
Random House 🏠 New York

Visit us on the Web!
SteppingStonesBooks.com
MagicTreeHouse.com

Educators and librarians, for a variety of teaching tools, visit us at
RHTeachersLibrarians.com

Library of Congress Cataloging-in-Publication Data
Osborne, Mary Pope.
Sharks and other predators / by Mary Pope Osborne and Natalie Pope Boyce ;
illustrated by Carlo Molinari.
p. cm. — (Magic tree house fact tracker)
"A nonfiction companion to Magic Tree House #53: Shadow of the Shark."
ISBN 978-0-385-38641-8 (trade) — ISBN 978-0-385-38642-5 (lib. bdg.) —
ISBN 978-0-385-38643-2 (ebook)
1. Predatory animals—Juvenile literature. 2. Sharks—Juvenile literature.
I. Boyce, Natalie Pope. II. Molinari, Carlo, illustrator. III. Title.
QL758.O755 2015 567'.3—dc23 2014029698

Printed in the United States of America
10 9 8 7 6 5 4 3 2 1

This book has been officially leveled by using the F&P Text Level Gradient™
Leveling System.

For Michael Dickens Pope
and members of the Greenbelt Land Trust

Scientific Consultant:
DR. JOHN A. SHIVIK, adjunct professor, Utah State University

Education Consultant:
HEIDI JOHNSON, language acquisition and science education specialist, Bisbee, Arizona

Special thanks to the great support from Random House: Heather Palisi; Mallory Loehr; Paula Sadler; Carlo Molinari for his great illustrations; and Diane Landolf, who manages to keep us safe no matter what

SHARKS AND
OTHER PREDATORS

Contents

1. Sharks and Other Predators   13

2. Sharks   27

3. Sharks as Predators   45

4. Cats, Large and Small   55

5. The Dog Family   73

6. Apex Predators   87

7. A Good Balance   103

Doing More Research   110

Index   118

Dear Readers,

In <u>Shadow of the Shark</u>, we went to the Caribbean Sea and had some thrilling adventures with a shark. Most people are afraid of sharks, but we wanted to know what they were really like. Learning the facts about things you're scared of can ease your fears.

We visited the library and checked out some great books. And then we sat down at a computer and did more research. We learned that predators are an important part of the food chain. Having them around helps the whole world to be healthy. We also found out that if one link of a food chain disappears—

whether it's a plant or an animal—many other living things can be at risk.

When we finished tracking the facts, we felt a lot better about all predators, from the largest to the smallest. It was so much fun finding out about predators that we wanted to share our knowledge with you. So get out your notebooks, and let's get to work!

Jack

Annie

1

Sharks and Other Predators

Sharks may be the most feared animals on earth. Some people even think that we'd be better off without them. What these people don't understand is that sharks and other predators (PRED-uh-turz) keep our planet healthy. And what's good for the planet is good for all of us.

Predators are animals that survive by eating other animals. They are not trying to be cruel. Predators must eat meat to stay alive.

Not all predators are scary. Lizards, frogs, and insects such as ladybugs and some other beetles are common predators. The creatures that they eat are their *prey*.

Many predators are also prey for other animals. For example, birds that eat worms

 Most ladybugs eat tiny insects such as this aphid.

are predators. Cats often prey on birds. And coyotes sometimes eat cats, so cats and birds can be both predators and prey.

What Types of Animals Are Predators?
Animals that depend on meat to survive are called *carnivores* (KAR-nuh-vorz). All carnivores are predators.

Animals that only eat plants, like cows and goats, are called <u>herbivores</u> (ER-buh-vorz).

The word <u>carnivore</u> comes from the Latin words <u>caro</u>, for meat, and <u>vorare</u>, which means <u>to devour</u>.

But many predators eat both plants and animals. They are called *omnivores* (OM-nuh-vorz). Humans are omnivores. Among the many other omnivores are bears, skunks, pigs, rats, and lizards.

Where Do Predators Live?

A habitat is a place where certain animals live, which has the climate, food, water, and plants they need to survive.

Predators live everywhere, in all kinds of *habitats*. Their homes are jungles, deserts, oceans, swamps, rivers, and steamy rain forests.

But you don't have to go far to see a predator. Look outside!

Have you ever heard the saying that the early bird gets the worm? Early in the morning, when the ground is cool and damp, earthworms often come up to the surface. Hungry robins stand by, waiting to gobble them up. The robin's good hearing and eyesight make it a deadly predator.

16

When robins cock their heads, they're listening and watching for earthworms.

Catching Their Prey

The bodies and brains of predators are made to catch their prey. This is called *adaptation*. Owls, for example, have adapted to hunt animals at night. Their big eyes help them see well in the dark. Tufts at the ends of their wings let them fly without making any noise.

Different predators hunt in different ways. Some stalk their prey by creeping

17

up on it. Leopards and other big cats are master stalkers. When they sneak up on their victims, they keep their heads down and their bodies close to the ground. Then they pounce with lightning speed!

Animals like cheetahs and wolves chase down their prey instead of stalking it.

Lions, bears, and many more predators often *scavenge* for food. This means that they will eat some dead animals that they find.

Other predators wait patiently to ambush their victims. Many are helped by their *camouflage* (KAA-muh-flahj). This means that their natural colors look the same as the world around them.

The boreal owl's feathers look like bark on trees, where it sits watching for mice. Arctic foxes have pure-white fur and are very hard to see in the snow.

Can you spot the arctic fox?

Why We Need Predators

All living things are connected by the food that they eat. This is called a food chain. Food chains are made up of plants and animals.

Plants are the first link in each chain. Plants gather and store energy from sunlight and water. Everything alive needs energy to grow and to stay healthy.

A food chain might look like this:

Sun and water give plants energy.

Insects eat the plants.

Green frogs eat the insects.

Great blue herons eat the green frogs.

Apex means the top of something. Animals such as gray wolves, leopards, and king cobras are at the top of their food chains. They are apex predators. No other animals prey on them.

Each link in the chain is necessary for the animals and plants above it. If plants die because of chemicals, disease, or lack of water, insects will also die. And then frogs, birds, and snakes will, too.

Because African lions can be dangerous, people kill them. Today there are fewer places where lions can live safely.

Lions have always preyed on baboons. Now that there are fewer lions, baboons have more places to live and are increasing in number.

Baboons are omnivores, eating both meat and plants.

Baboons carry diseases that spread to other animals, including people. They also destroy property and eat crops. Now parts of Africa have way too many baboons.

How Predators Find Their Prey
Predators depend on their senses to find prey. Sight, hearing, taste, smell, and touch are super-important for hunting.

Birds, for example, have eyes on either side of their heads so they can see in all directions.

Pelicans can spot fish from sixty feet in the air and dive straight down to grab them.

A powerful sense of smell is also helpful. Snakes constantly flick their tongues in and out of their mouths to pick up the smells around them. Bears may have the best sense of smell of any animal. Polar bears can smell a seal hiding under three feet of ice!

Nature depends on the right balance between predators and prey. This balance keeps nature healthy and stops one species from taking over. Without a good balance, life on our planet might not even exist.

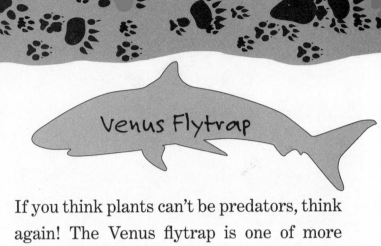

Venus Flytrap

If you think plants can't be predators, think again! The Venus flytrap is one of more than 500 different kinds of predator plants. It feeds on spiders, caterpillars, slugs, flies, and crickets.

The leaves of the Venus flytrap give off nectar that attracts bugs. The leaves are loaded with tiny hairs that sense movement. When an insect walks on them, the leaves snap shut, trapping the bug inside. Then the flytrap sends out a special acid to dissolve the insect. After several days, the flytrap opens its leaves and the outer skeleton of the insect falls out. The flytrap is ready for another meal!

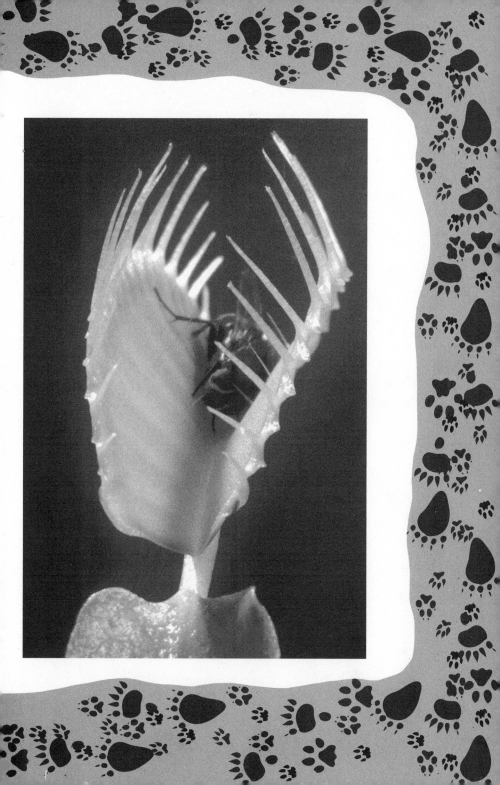

2

Sharks

Sharks are among the oldest creatures on earth. Their very first relatives appeared over 400 million years ago, long before dinosaurs roamed the earth. About a million years ago, most sharks began to look like the ones we know today. Now there are over 400 different kinds of sharks.

Some sharks lay eggs, while others have live births. Most live for twenty to thirty years, but whale sharks and spiny dogfish

Spiny dogfish shark

sharks can make it to a hundred years old!

And not all sharks eat meat. Basking sharks, megamouth sharks, and whale sharks are huge animals that live only on plankton.

Size

Sharks come in different sizes. The largest are whale sharks. They grow to sixty feet

Plankton are tiny plants and animals floating in the water. (This photograph has been magnified many times.)

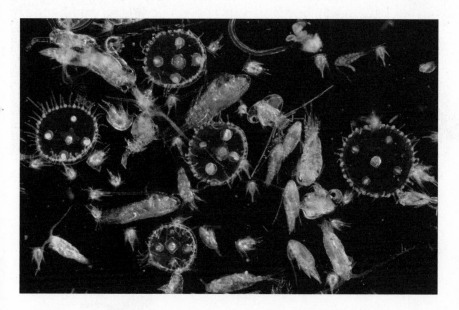

and weigh over 40,000 pounds! These slow-moving sharks have mouths about five feet wide with over 300 rows of little teeth!

Many sharks are three feet long or

shorter. The spined pygmy shark is among the smallest. This shark is about eight to ten inches long and lives in the deep sea. Its stomach lights up in the dark water, probably as a way to attract prey.

This is how small a person is compared to a whale shark.

Larger sharks, like great whites and hammerheads, can be over twenty feet long. On average, however, most sharks are about five to twelve feet in length.

Hammerhead sharks use their heads to butt stingrays and hold them down on the ocean floor.

31

Habitat

Sharks live in oceans everywhere, especially in the warmer waters of the equator. Some, like the Pacific sleeper shark, the blue shark, and the Greenland sleeper shark, are at home in cold waters.

 The Greenland sleeper shark can live under the ice.

Although most sharks live in salt water, bull sharks and river sharks exist in both salt and fresh water.

Many sharks migrate, or travel long distances from where they usually live. It's possible that they do this to mate or find food. Great whites, for example, are known to swim thousands of miles every year from the coast of South Africa to Australia.

Streamlined!

Sharks have bodies adapted for swimming. They are narrower at their heads and their tails. Their streamlined shape cuts through the water easily. The shortfin mako shark swims the fastest. It can reach speeds of about twenty miles per hour.

As sharks glide through the water, powerful tails known as caudal fins move from side to side to push them ahead. Two

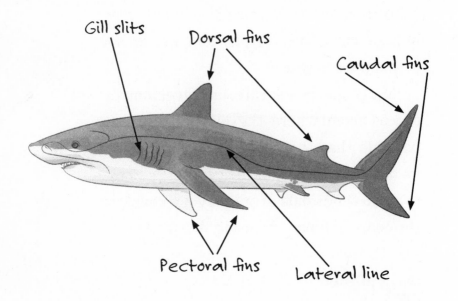

Gill slits

Dorsal fins

Caudal fins

Pectoral fins

Lateral line

Sharks can't swim backward.

dorsal fins on their backs keep them steady, while pectoral, or side, fins lift them up.

Cartilage and Livers

Most fish have skeletons made of bone and *cartilage* (KAR-tuh-lidge). Cartilage is tissue that feels hard but is lighter and more flexible than bone. A shark's skeleton is made only of cartilage.

Human skeletons are both bone and cartilage.

Cartilage helps sharks turn quickly and keeps them from sinking to the bottom of the ocean.

Most fish have gas-filled bladders to stay afloat. Sharks don't have these. Instead, they have large, oily livers. Oil is lighter than water. If sharks keep swimming, this oil will keep them from sinking.

Breathing

Unlike dolphins, sharks don't go to the surface to breathe. They breathe underwater. Rather than breathing through lungs, sharks and other fish breathe through gills. There are five to seven pairs of gill slits on either side of a shark's head. Water flows into the gill slits to get

35

Great white shark

Gills

to the gills. The gills take oxygen from the water and send it throughout the shark's body.

Skin

A shark's skin is about four inches thick and protects it from injuries.

Because the skin is made up of small scales that look like tiny teeth, it feels like sandpaper. These are called *placoid* scales.

The scales point back toward the shark's tail. If you stroke a shark from its head to its tail, it doesn't hurt. Just don't try running your hands from its tail to its head! Ouch!

As sharks move forward, their scales channel water backward and help them go faster.

Camouflage

Many sharks are darker on top and lighter underneath. This is their special camouflage. They are hard to spot from above the water because their darker colors are the same as the water's.

Sunlight shines down through the water.

Since the underneath of a shark's body is
lighter, fish swimming below have a hard
time seeing a shark's white belly in the sun-
lit water.

Jaws and Teeth
Sharks have very powerful jaws. Their
teeth point backward to give them a strong
grip. Right before they attack, their jaws
unhinge and move forward.

The great white has about fifty teeth at one time. It can have as many as 50,000 teeth in its lifetime!

Sharks often lose teeth, but their bodies are always making new ones. When a tooth falls out, another one moves up to take its place.

Most sharks have five or more rows of teeth.

Different kinds of sharks have different kinds of teeth. Scientists can usually tell the kind of shark by the shape of its teeth.

Sharks' teeth are adapted to their diets. A great white's teeth are jagged triangles

Tiger shark tooth

Mako shark tooth

Great white shark tooth

for tearing and ripping. Lemon and mako sharks have narrow teeth with sawlike edges to hold on to slippery fish. Sharks that eat crabs and shellfish have thick back teeth for crunching shells.

This nurse shark uses its thick back teeth to chomp on a Caribbean spiny lobster.

Megalodon—Yikes!

Scientists usually learn about early animals by studying fossils of their skeletons. Shark cartilage often dissolves before the skeletons can become fossils. Sharks' teeth are made from a hard mineral, not cartilage. The best fossils of ancient sharks are their teeth.

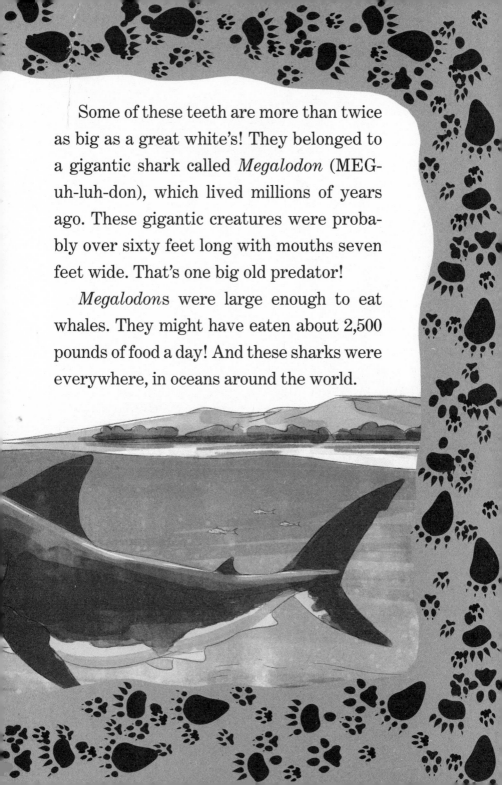

Some of these teeth are more than twice as big as a great white's! They belonged to a gigantic shark called *Megalodon* (MEG-uh-luh-don), which lived millions of years ago. These gigantic creatures were probably over sixty feet long with mouths seven feet wide. That's one big old predator!

*Megalodon*s were large enough to eat whales. They might have eaten about 2,500 pounds of food a day! And these sharks were everywhere, in oceans around the world.

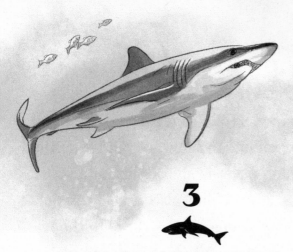

3

Sharks as Predators

Their great hunting skills have helped sharks survive for so long. They are born to track down animals like fish, seals, sea lions, squids, turtles, octopuses, dolphins, shellfish, birds, and even other sharks. As sharks patrol the ocean, all of their senses are on high alert.

Lateral Line
One of the most amazing things that sharks and other fish have is a *lateral line*. This

line of nerves runs along both sides of the shark up to its head. The nerves pick up movements in the water and send this information to the shark's brain.

The lateral line also detects smells. When any animal swims through the water, its smell is left behind in a trail. This is very helpful to a hungry shark!

Smell

Sharks don't use their noses for breathing. Nostrils under their snouts are for smelling. A shark's sense of smell is the strongest of all its senses.

Great whites have the largest olfactory bulb of all sharks.

Water flowing through the nostrils carries different odors along with it. These smells go to an olfactory bulb. This is a part of the brain that tells the shark what is making a smell.

Many experts think sharks can smell their prey from as far as several football fields away. And some sharks might even smell a single drop of blood in water that would fill an Olympic-sized swimming pool!

Hearing

Sharks' ears are small openings behind their eyes. They can hear something moving from several miles away. Despite the small size of sharks' ears, they pick up even the slightest sounds.

Sharks often prey on sick or injured fish. They listen for those that are splashing or swimming slowly or unevenly. By eating unhealthy fish, sharks keep the water cleaner and stop diseases from spreading to other fish.

Sight

Sharks see as well at night as during the day. Because their eyes are spaced far apart on either side of their heads, they have a very wide view. In clear water, they can spot something up to one hundred feet away.

The frilled shark has special catlike eyes so it can see in the deep, dark ocean. It's very much like sharks that lived 350 million years ago!

When sharks attack, they risk hurting their eyes. To keep them safe, sharks roll their eyes back into their sockets. Then they use a special organ system near their eyes called the ampullae of Lorenzini (am-PUH-lee of lor-un-ZEE-nee) to tell them where their prey is. With their eyes closed, they can "see" what their prey is doing.

The ampullae of Lorenzini are canals in the shark's head. They are filled with jelly-like material that senses electrical currents made by moving animals.

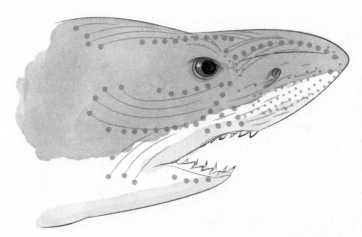

Attacks on Humans

Sharks almost never attack people. You are more likely to be conked on the head by a coconut or struck by lightning or caught in an avalanche than attacked by a shark!

 Beaches in South Africa and Australia have nets that protect swimmers from sharks.

Sharks are actually shy. When they attack people, it's often by mistake. They're drawn to anything splashing in the ocean, even a swimmer's kicking legs. Remember the injured, splashing fish?

It's always better to swim during the day, because many sharks hunt at night. It's also better to swim in a group and stay away from sandbars, because sharks sometimes look for fish there. The best thing to do, however, is to enjoy being at the beach with your friends!

Mystery: Who Killed the Great White?

In 2003, scientists in Australia tagged a nine-foot great white shark. The tag was to record how deep it swam and what its temperature was.

Sometime later, the tag without the shark washed up on an Australian beach. It showed that the shark had been 1,900 feet down in the ocean. It also said that the temperature had been forty-six degrees. But then it suddenly shot up to seventy-eight degrees. It stayed that way for eight days.

Scientists now think that a larger animal dragged the shark down in the cold deep ocean. The high temperature was from inside its attacker's stomach.

What animal is big enough to eat a nine-foot shark? What animal's stomach is around seventy-eight degrees? Experts are pretty sure the predator was a killer whale!

4

Cats, Large and Small

Cats might be the ultimate predators. They are born with flexible bodies, powerful legs, and great hunting instincts. Cats are expert runners, climbers, and jumpers.

Instincts are natural ways of acting that animals are born with.

The very first cats appeared about 25 million years ago. The most famous early cat is the Smilodon, or saber-toothed cat. This fierce animal had canine teeth nearly a foot long. It feasted on prey as large as woolly mammoths!

 Canine teeth are long, pointed teeth that meat-eaters have in the front of their mouths. They are used for holding down prey and for fighting.

Different Cats

Today there are about thirty-six different species, or kinds, of wild cats. They come in all different sizes. The largest is the Siberian tiger, which can weigh over 700 pounds. One of the smallest is the black-footed cat of Africa. Males weigh a little over four pounds.

Some Very
Cool Cats

tiger
lion
jaguar
leopard
cougar
cheetah
lynx
ocelot
bobcat

Habitats

Wild cats live on every continent except Antarctica and Australia. Most species thrive where there are plenty of trees. Many live in warm climates, but others survive well in cold weather.

 Although most cats don't live in groups, lions hang out in families called prides.

Jaguars (JAG-warz) roam the steamy jungles of South and Central America. Lions, often called the kings of the jungle, don't live in jungles. Their homes are on the hot, dry African savannas, or plains, and in a dry forest in India. Snow leopards wander the high mountains of central Asia, while cougars live all the way from southeastern Alaska down to Argentina.

Cougars are also known as pumas or mountain lions.

Diet

The cat family is super-carnivorous! Cats need the protein and fat from meat more than any other land animal. Their bodies also need calcium, which they get from eating bones.

Crunching on bones also keeps their teeth and gums healthy.

Cats use their long, sharp canine teeth to grab their prey and kill it quickly. They

59

often kill an animal and hide it so they can feast on it for several days.

Large cats like tigers, cougars, and lions eat an amazing amount of meat. Cougars average about ten pounds a day. Tigers can feast on twenty pounds at one time!

All cats have rough, raspy tongues that strip skin off the bones of their prey.

 Cats often lick themselves and each other to stay clean!

Paws and Claws

Many cats can run fast for short distances. But it's really hard to beat a cheetah. It can go from zero to seventy miles per hour in just seconds! That's as fast as a speeding car!

Cheetahs use their tails to keep their balance when they make sharp turns.

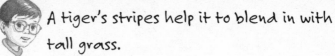 A tiger's stripes help it to blend in with tall grass.

Cats have five claws on their front feet and four on the back. The front claws are sharper, for bringing down and holding prey. Their claws also help them climb

62

trees. (And their strong legs make them great swimmers!)

Fur

Cats in cold climates have thicker fur. They also have tufts of hair between their toes to keep them from slipping on the ice.

A cat's fur can be great camouflage, especially if it has patterns on it. Leopards, jaguars, and cheetahs have dark spots on their light coats. This makes them hard to see when they hide in trees or tall grass. Their spots fade into the shadows, and the light-colored fur blends into the sunlight.

Did you know that no two tigers have exactly the same pattern on their coats?

Lions can be hard to see as well. Their light brown fur is a lot like the colors of dry African plains. And on snowy mountain

63

peaks, a snow leopard's white coat makes it almost invisible.

Sight, Hearing, and Smell

Cats sleep during the day and hunt at night. Their eyes are adapted for seeing in the dark.

They also have excellent hearing. When a noise interests them, their ears swivel toward the sound. They can pick up high-pitched noises that no humans can hear.

Cats also have a great sense of smell. There's a scent organ on the roof of their mouths called the Jacobson's organ. Their tongues carry smells to this organ and on to their brains.

Touch

Cats have whiskers on their mouths, noses, chins, eyes, and even legs. Their whiskers tell them a lot. The base of a whisker is full of nerve endings. If a cat is trying to move through an opening, its whiskers tell it if it will fit.

Whiskers are especially helpful in the dark.

Cats can't see their prey up close. Their whiskers close around their noses like a basket. They help them sense where their

Cat Noises!
Both wild cats and house cats make a lot of different sounds. Here are some ways that they communicate:

Spit!

Watch out! I'm ready for you!

I am REALLY getting annoyed with you!

Grr!

Hiss!

I can seriously, totally defend myself!

prey is. They act much like the ampullae of Lorenzini on sharks.

Cats and People

Today cats are the most popular pets of all. They were probably first tamed over 12,000 years ago. That's when people in the Middle East became farmers. Mice and rats were eating grain in their storehouses. Farmers probably kept wild cats to eat these pesky creatures.

About 4,000 years ago, Egyptians worshiped a cat goddess. They also kept cats in their houses. There are even mummified bodies of cats in some tombs. But that's not all: there is an ancient cat cemetery in Egypt with over 300,000 cat mummies!

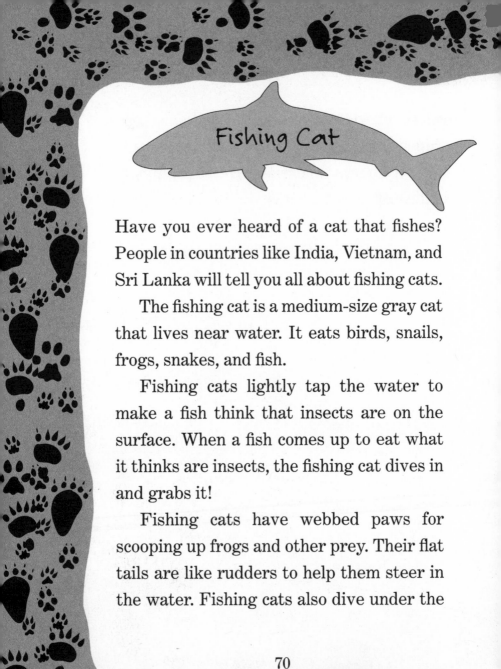

Fishing Cat

Have you ever heard of a cat that fishes? People in countries like India, Vietnam, and Sri Lanka will tell you all about fishing cats.

The fishing cat is a medium-size gray cat that lives near water. It eats birds, snails, frogs, snakes, and fish.

Fishing cats lightly tap the water to make a fish think that insects are on the surface. When a fish comes up to eat what it thinks are insects, the fishing cat dives in and grabs it!

Fishing cats have webbed paws for scooping up frogs and other prey. Their flat tails are like rudders to help them steer in the water. Fishing cats also dive under the water to surprise and catch birds floating on the surface. If you ever lose your fishing pole, maybe invite a fishing cat to hang out with you!

5

The Dog Family

If you've ever heard wolves howling on a cold winter night, you'll never forget it. Wolves belong to the dog family. All animals in this family are called canids. Different members of the dog family live on every continent except Antarctica.

There are about thirty-five different members of the dog family. Among them are coyotes, jackals, foxes, dholes, and both wild and tame dogs. Many of them have ears that stand up, long legs, bushy tails, and long, slim snouts, or muzzles.

The gray wolf is the largest and can weigh from 50 pounds to over 100 pounds. The little Blanford's fox weighs just over two pounds.

Gray wolf

Blanford's fox

Habitats

Canids make their homes in mountains, grasslands, forests, and scorching deserts.

Red foxes live in eighty-three countries on five continents. Gray wolves are found in sixty-five countries in North America, Europe, and Asia. These two species are in more places than any other canid.

Africa, Asia, and South America have the largest number of species of canids.

Bodies

Most animals in the dog family have long legs and can run for a long time.

Gray wolves are close relatives of our pet dogs.

African wild dogs often run about forty miles per hour for up to an hour at a time.

Wolves trot more than they walk. A trot is halfway between a walk and a run. They trot at about eight miles per hour and are known to cover sixty miles in a single night!

Although wolves and coyotes can travel for hours at a good pace, they run very fast only when they are close to their prey.

All canids have a powerful sense of smell. Their long muzzles hold as many as 300 million scent receptors!

People only have about 5 million scent receptors.

They usually have excellent hearing as well. Bat-eared foxes in Africa mainly live on termites. These small foxes' ears are over five inches long. They can hear termites chewing!

Diet

Canids eat many different things. Wolves are strict carnivores. Although they often

Foxes surprise their prey by
pouncing on it.

scavenge for food, they also hunt deer,
moose, caribou, mice, and birds.

Other canids, like jackals and maned
wolves, survive on small animals, insects,
plants, and fruit. Coyotes eat just about

anything they can find, including lambs, sheep, birds, frogs, and berries. Sometimes farmers see them in fields munching on a juicy watermelon! Black-backed jackals in South Africa eat meat, but they also love snacking on pineapples!

Behavior

Many canids, like gray wolves, wild dogs, and coyotes, live in family groups called packs. Packs give each animal a better chance of survival.

Wolf packs usually have seven or eight members.

Although wolves sometimes hunt alone or in pairs, they also hunt in packs. By working together, they can bring down animals much larger than themselves, such as moose or caribou.

The leader of the wolf pack is the most powerful male. He is called the alpha male. His mate is the alpha female. Alpha males and females are usually the only wolves in a pack that mate and have pups. The rest of the pack helps feed and protect the pups.

Communication

Wolves, coyotes, and dogs show feelings through their body language. When they feel unsure or threatened, hairs, or hackles, on their shoulders stand up.

If an alpha wolf is annoyed with another wolf, he'll stare into its eyes for a long time. This means "Watch it, Buster!"

Coyotes, wolves, and dogs howl to tell their packs where they are. Wolves also moan, growl, and yelp. Foxes scream

This wolf has its hackles raised.

when they're in trouble. They sound like people!

Sometimes coyotes yip and howl together. This tells other coyotes to stay away from their territory. They sound like a crazy coyote chorus!

Endangered Canids

Some canids, such as dholes, maned wolves, and African wild dogs, are endangered species and might not survive.

 Dholes, or Indian wild dogs, can jump twelve feet high and leap distances of up to twenty feet!

Ethiopian wolves are the only wolves left in Africa. They are the most endangered of all the dog family. They look a lot like coyotes and live in large, close-knit packs high in the mountains of Ethiopia.

Because of rabies and loss of habitat, there are fewer than 500 Ethiopian wolves left. Once these beautiful animals disappear, they will be gone forever.

Turn the page to find out about wolves in Yellowstone.

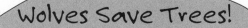
Wolves Save Trees!

Because wolves ate cattle, deer, elk, and sheep, people began hunting them in and around Yellowstone National Park. By 1926, there were none left. Over the years, scientists saw that cottonwood and willow trees in the park had stopped growing along the riverbanks. Elk were eating all of the young shoots before they could grow into trees.

In 1995, wildlife experts brought wolves back to the Yellowstone area. To their surprise, the trees began growing again. Elk were no longer eating the shoots. When elk stood by the river, they were out in the open without protection. With wolves around, they needed to be harder to see. They could not stand around eating shoots. So now, thanks to the wolves, there are plenty of cottonwoods and willows in Yellowstone!

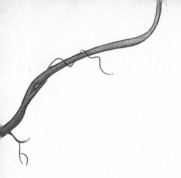

6

Apex Predators

Animals at the very top of a food chain are known as apex predators. Apex predators can be as small as a tiny ant.

Army ants in central and east Africa are fierce predators. An ant on its own might not seem dangerous, but a swarm of army ants are as powerful as a tiger. When thousands of these ants are on the move looking for a new home, they cover trees, bushes, and jungle paths. They even march through houses. Nothing can stop them.

They will eat just about any living thing. Their mandibles, or jaws, deliver a painful bite. Once the ants catch something, they dissolve it by spreading acid over its body.

Army ants usually prey on insects. But when a huge swarm comes, people rush their animals to safety. Snakes, insects, birds, lizards—nothing that moves is safe from the ants.

Electric eel

There are other unusual animals in the apex group. Electric eels are apex predators living in the Amazon and Orinoco Rivers of South America. These fish give off such powerful electrical shocks that they can easily kill other fish and possibly even humans. They shoot out enough electricity to light up twelve lightbulbs!

Some animals that you'd think are apex predators actually aren't. The giant squid has a huge, sharp beak and eyes the size of basketballs, and can be sixty feet long. But the giant squid has a major predator. And that's the sperm whale.

Sperm whales spend much of their time deep in the ocean. Although they have big

Sperm whale

teeth, they don't chew their prey. They suck it down instead!

Apex predators are an important part of balancing a food chain. If even one of them or their prey should disappear, it could change how the entire food chain works.

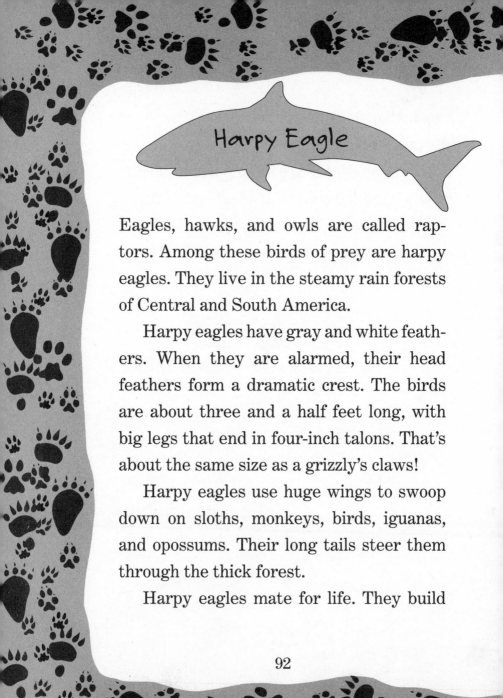

Harpy Eagle

Eagles, hawks, and owls are called raptors. Among these birds of prey are harpy eagles. They live in the steamy rain forests of Central and South America.

Harpy eagles have gray and white feathers. When they are alarmed, their head feathers form a dramatic crest. The birds are about three and a half feet long, with big legs that end in four-inch talons. That's about the same size as a grizzly's claws!

Harpy eagles use huge wings to swoop down on sloths, monkeys, birds, iguanas, and opossums. Their long tails steer them through the thick forest.

Harpy eagles mate for life. They build

giant twig nests five feet long and four feet deep, lined with soft green plants and animal fur. The eagles often use the same nests year after year.

Leopard Seal

Leopard seals are fierce apex predators in Antarctica. They have strong jaws and large mouths lined with very sharp teeth. The seals eat krill, penguins, squid, and fish. They are the only seal that eats other seals.

They can grow to be twelve feet long. Their big front flippers push them through the water with great force. Leopard seals reach speeds of twenty-four miles per hour

in the water. They can turn quickly and dive hundreds of feet below the surface.

The seals hide under the ice, waiting for penguins or other seals to slip into the water. Penguins don't stand a chance. Not only are these seals stronger, but they can also swim faster!

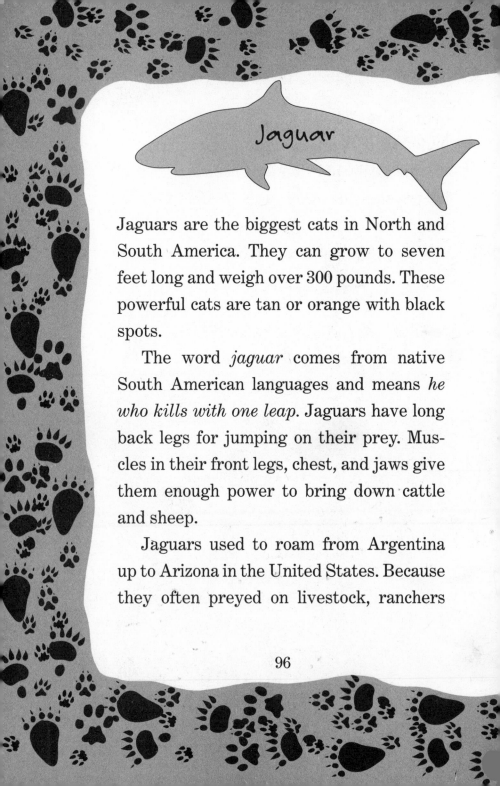

Jaguar

Jaguars are the biggest cats in North and South America. They can grow to seven feet long and weigh over 300 pounds. These powerful cats are tan or orange with black spots.

The word *jaguar* comes from native South American languages and means *he who kills with one leap*. Jaguars have long back legs for jumping on their prey. Muscles in their front legs, chest, and jaws give them enough power to bring down cattle and sheep.

Jaguars used to roam from Argentina up to Arizona in the United States. Because they often preyed on livestock, ranchers killed off many of them. Although there are jaguar sightings in different places, today they are mostly found in far-off corners of Central America and South America near the Amazon basin.

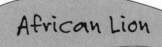

African Lion

African lions often live in groups of three males, twelve females, and their cubs. The males guard the pride and watch for intruders. The females hunt and tend to the cubs.

Lions sleep about sixteen hours a day. Sometimes they lie on their backs with their feet up in the air. Sometimes they take naps lying on a tree branch.

The females hunt at night. They prey on antelopes, zebras, wild dogs, and other animals. When the lionesses corner their prey, they make a half circle around it before going in for the kill.

When lions gather to share a meal, the males get first choice, then the females, and finally the cubs.

Then, after they eat, they usually lie down for . . . you guessed it! Another good, long sleep!

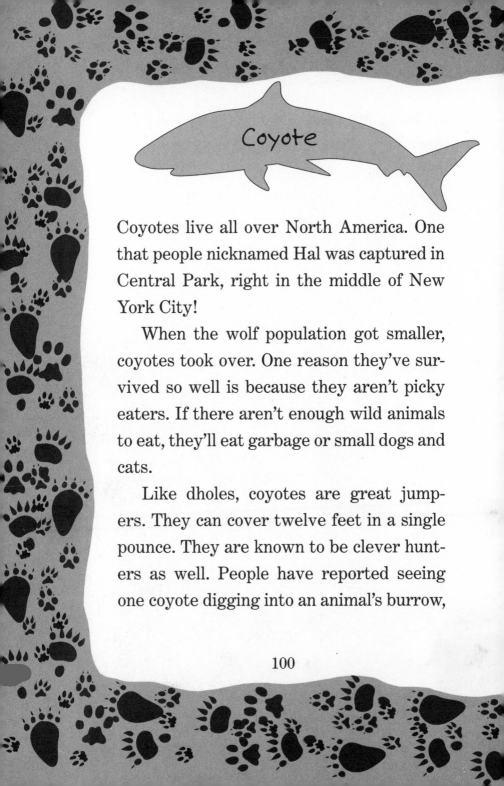

Coyote

Coyotes live all over North America. One that people nicknamed Hal was captured in Central Park, right in the middle of New York City!

When the wolf population got smaller, coyotes took over. One reason they've survived so well is because they aren't picky eaters. If there aren't enough wild animals to eat, they'll eat garbage or small dogs and cats.

Like dholes, coyotes are great jumpers. They can cover twelve feet in a single pounce. They are known to be clever hunters as well. People have reported seeing one coyote digging into an animal's burrow, while others waited at the opposite end for it to escape.

Although millions of coyotes have been killed because they prey on livestock, they still continue to thrive. There might even be some where you live.

7

A Good Balance

Animals and plants are all closely connected. Each is important for the survival of the others. There has to be a good balance between predators and prey. There also has to be a good balance between animals and plants.

Trees are good for many things. They lower the temperature, put oxygen in the air, and make homes for birds and other creatures.

When cottonwoods began growing along

the riverbanks in Yellowstone again, their shade cooled the water. Trout prefer cooler water. Beavers eat cottonwood trees and use them for building their lodges. These animals increased, and so did songbirds and frogs.

If one species of predators disappears, the number of animals it would have eaten can get out of control. After people began killing sharks off the coast of Jamaica, algae increased, taking over the coral reefs. Sharks around Jamaica used to eat more groupers. As sharks disappeared, groupers took over and ate most of the small fish.

Grouper

When sharks were plentiful, small fish had eaten the algae and kept the reefs healthy. But with fewer sharks, larger fish began to eat the smaller ones. When that happened, there were not enough little fish left to eat the algae.

Sea otters

Sea otters off the coast of Alaska were hunted until very few were left. Sea urchins living in the waters there had been a big part of their diet.

When otters disappeared, the number of sea urchins began to grow. They ate up most of the kelp that other sea creatures depended

Healthy kelp surrounds this sea otter in the ocean near Alaska.

on for food. When the otters were brought back, the kelp forests returned as well.

A Hard Life

Predators use their incredible hunting skills to stay alive. But as skilled as they are, they also need a little luck to catch their prey.

It's not easy being a predator. For one thing, it's hard to catch enough food. Lions, for example, bring down their prey only one out of three times. Foxes have been known to hunt all day just to carry a single mouse back to their dens. Cheetahs catch their prey only about half the time.

Luckily for them, wolves and other predators are able to go for a long time without eating. Great white sharks will eat sixty-six pounds of meat at one time and then go for weeks without food. Some snakes can wait for six months between meals! Lions have a feast and then sleep for several days.

Saving Predators

Nature needs a good balance between animals and plants. Predators and prey are key to keeping this balance. It's important to save animals like tigers, polar bears, giant otters, leopards, and cheetahs, all of which are in danger of disappearing.

If they are gone forever, then the animals and plants in their food chains might also be at risk. All of us need a world with beautiful trees, clean oceans, and healthy plants and animals. We can thank predators for giving us many of these gifts. We can also work to make sure that great white sharks, tigers, lions, wolves, and all the rest of them are around for many years to come.

Doing More Research

There's a lot more you can learn about predators. The fun of research is seeing how many different sources you can explore.

Books

Most libraries and bookstores have books about predators.

Here are some things to remember when you're using books for research:

1. You don't have to read the whole book. Check the table of contents and the index to find the topics you're interested in.

2. Write down the name of the book.

When you take notes, make sure you write down the name of the book in your notebook so you can find it again.

3. Never copy exactly from a book.

When you learn something new from a book, put it in your own words.

4. Make sure the book is <u>nonfiction</u>.

Some books tell make-believe stories about predators. Make-believe stories are called *fiction*. They're fun to read, but not good for research.

Research books have facts and tell true stories. They are called *nonfiction*. A librarian or teacher can help you make sure the books you use for research are nonfiction.

Here are some good nonfiction books about predators:

- *Big Cats* by Seymour Simon
- *Everything Big Cats*, National Geographic Kids series, by Elizabeth Carney
- *Mission: Wolf Rescue*, National Geographic Kids series, by Kitson Jazynka
- *Shark*, a DK Eyewitness Book, by Miranda MacQuitty
- *Sharks!* by Ginjer L. Clarke
- *Wolves* by Seymour Simon

Aquariums and Zoos

Many aquariums and zoos can help you learn more about predators.

When you go to an aquarium or zoo:

1. Be sure to take your notebook!
Write down anything that catches your interest. Draw pictures, too!

2. Ask questions.
There are almost always people at aquariums and zoos who can help you find what you're looking for.

3. Check the calendar.
Many aquariums and zoos have special events and activities just for kids!

Here are some aquariums and zoos that have predators:

- Aquarium of the Pacific (Long Beach, California)
- National Aquarium (Baltimore)
- New York Aquarium
- Saint Louis Zoo (Missouri)
- San Diego Zoo (California)
- Shedd Aquarium (Chicago)
- The Smithsonian's National Zoo (Washington, D.C.)

DVDs

There are some great nonfiction DVDs about predators. As with books, make sure the DVDs you watch for research are nonfiction!

Check your library or video store for these and other nonfiction titles about predators:

- *Discovery Channel Shark DVD Set* from the Discovery Channel
- *Super Predators* from National Geographic Classics
- *Ultimate Cat* from National Geographic

The Internet

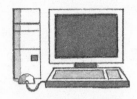

Many websites have facts about sharks and other predators. Some also have games and activities that can help make learning about predators even more fun.

Ask your teacher or your parents to help you find more websites like these:

- enchantedlearning.com/subjects /mammals/tiger
- kids.nationalgeographic.com/animals /gray-wolf
- kids.sandiegozoo.org/animals
- kidzone.ws/sharks
- nationalzoo.si.edu/Animals/AsiaTrail /CloudedLeopard/factsheet.cfm

- sciencekids.co.nz/sciencefacts/animals /shark.html

Good luck!

Index

African wild dogs, 75,
82
ampullae of Lorenzini,
49, 67
apex predators, 20,
87–101
arctic foxes, 18, 19
army ants, 87–88

baboons, 21–22
basking sharks, 28
bat-eared foxes, 76
bears, 16, 18, 23, 108
birds, 14–15, 16–17, 18,
21, 22, 23, 45, 70,
71, 77, 78, 88, 92–93,
94–95, 103, 104
black-backed jackals,
78
black-footed cats, 56
Blanford's foxes, 74

blue sharks, 32
boreal owls, 18
bull sharks, 33

camouflage, 18, 37–38,
62, 63, 64
carnivores, 15, 59, 76
cartilage, 34–35, 42
cats, 15, 18, 55–71,
96–99, 100, 107, 108
claws of, 61–63
diet of, 59–60
fur of, 63–64
habitats of, 57–58
noises of, 66–67
people and, 21,
68–69
senses of, 64–65
species of, 56–57
tails of, 61, 70
teeth of, 55, 56, 59

tongues of, 60, 64
whiskers of, 64–67
cheetahs, 18, 61, 63,
    107, 108
cougars, 58, 59, 60
coyotes, 15, 73, 76,
    77–78, 79, 80, 81,
    83, 100–101

dholes, 73, 82, 100
dogs, 73–85, 98, 100–101
  communication by,
    80–81
  diet of, 76–78
  habitats of, 75
  packs of, 79–80
  senses of, 76
  tails of, 74

Egypt, 69
electric eels, 89
endangered species,
    82–83, 108

Ethiopian wolves, 83

fish, 23, 34–35, 38, 41,
    45, 47, 51, 70–71,
    89, 94, 104–105
fishing cats, 70–71
food chains, 19–22,
    87–91, 108
fossils, 42–43
foxes, 18, 19, 73, 74,
    75, 76, 77, 81,
    107
frilled sharks, 48

giant squids, 90
gray wolves, 20, 74,
    75, 79
great white sharks,
    31, 33, 36, 39, 40, 43,
    46, 52–53, 107–108
Greenland sleeper
    sharks, 32
groupers, 104–105

hammerhead sharks, 31

harpy eagles, 92–93

herbivores, 15

insects, 14, 21, 24, 70, 77, 88

jackals, 73, 77, 78

Jacobson's organ, 64

jaguars, 58, 63, 96–97

killer whales, 53

king cobras, 20

lateral line, 45–46

lemon sharks, 41

leopard seals, 94–95

leopards, 18, 20, 58, 63, 64, 108

lions, 18, 21, 45, 57, 58, 60, 63, 98–99, 107, 108

mako sharks, 33, 40, 41

maned wolves, 77, 82

Megalodon, 42–43

megamouth sharks, 28

nurse sharks, 41

olfactory bulbs, 46

omnivores, 16, 21

otters, 105–107, 108

owls, 17, 18, 92

Pacific sleeper sharks, 32

pelicans, 23

placoid scales, 37

plankton, 28, 29

polar bears, 23, 108

red foxes, 75

river sharks, 33

scavengers, 18, 77

seals, 23, 45, 94–95
senses, 22–23, 45–49,
    64–65, 76
sharks, 13, 27–53, 67,
    104–105, 107–108
  fins of, 33–34
  gills of, 35–36
  habitats of, 32–33
  livers of, 35
  migration of, 33
  people and, 13,
    50–51, 104
  senses of, 45–49
  shape of, 33–34
  size of, 28–31
  skin of, 36–37
  tails of, 33, 37
  teeth of, 29, 38–41,
    42–43
Siberian tigers, 56
Smilodons, 55
snakes, 20, 21, 23, 70,
    88, 108

snow leopards, 58, 64
sperm whales, 90–91
spined pygmy sharks,
    30
spiny dogfish sharks,
    27, 28

tiger sharks, 40
tigers, 56, 60, 62, 63,
    87, 108

Venus flytraps, 24

whale sharks, 27,
    28–29, 30
whales, 43, 90–91
wolves, 18, 20, 73–85,
    100, 107, 108

Yellowstone National
    Park, 84–85, 104

Photographs courtesy of:

Have you read the adventure that
matches up with this book?

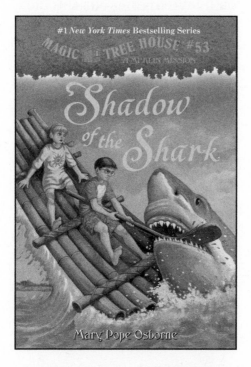

Don't miss Magic Tree House® #53
Shadow of the Shark
Jack and Annie dive into danger when
the magic tree house whisks them away
to shark-infested waters!

If you liked Magic Tree House® #15:
Viking Ships at Sunrise,
you'll love finding out the facts
behind the fiction in

Magic Tree House®
Fact Tracker

VIKINGS

A nonfiction companion to
Magic Tree House® #15:
Viking Ships at Sunrise

It's Jack and Annie's very own guide
to the Viking Age.

Coming soon!

Don't miss Magic Tree House® Super Edition #1: *Danger in the Darkest Hour*

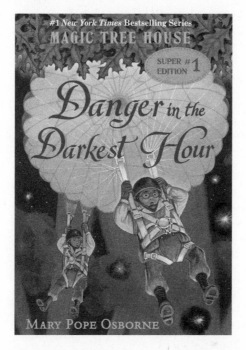

Jack and Annie travel to Normandy, France, during World War II for their most dangerous mission ever!

Magic Tree House® Books

#1: Dinosaurs Before Dark
#2: The Knight at Dawn
#3: Mummies in the Morning
#4: Pirates Past Noon
#5: Night of the Ninjas
#6: Afternoon on the Amazon
#7: Sunset of the Sabertooth
#8: Midnight on the Moon
#9: Dolphins at Daybreak
#10: Ghost Town at Sundown
#11: Lions at Lunchtime
#12: Polar Bears Past Bedtime
#13: Vacation Under the Volcano
#14: Day of the Dragon King
#15: Viking Ships at Sunrise
#16: Hour of the Olympics
#17: Tonight on the *Titanic*
#18: Buffalo Before Breakfast
#19: Tigers at Twilight
#20: Dingoes at Dinnertime
#21: Civil War on Sunday
#22: Revolutionary War on Wednesday
#23: Twister on Tuesday
#24: Earthquake in the Early Morning
#25: Stage Fright on a Summer Night
#26: Good Morning, Gorillas
#27: Thanksgiving on Thursday
#28: High Tide in Hawaii

#42: A Good Night for Ghosts
#43: Leprechaun in Late Winter
#44: A Ghost Tale for Christmas Time
#45: A Crazy Day with Cobras
#46: Dogs in the Dead of Night
#47: Abe Lincoln at Last!
#48: A Perfect Time for Pandas
#49: Stallion by Starlight
#50: Hurry Up, Houdini!
#51: High Time for Heroes
#52: Soccer on Sunday
#53: Shadow of the Shark

Merlin Missions

#29: Christmas in Camelot
#30: Haunted Castle on Hallows Eve
#31: Summer of the Sea Serpent
#32: Winter of the Ice Wizard
#33: Carnival at Candlelight
#34: Season of the Sandstorms
#35: Night of the New Magicians
#36: Blizzard of the Blue Moon
#37: Dragon of the Red Dawn
#38: Monday with a Mad Genius
#39: Dark Day in the Deep Sea
#40: Eve of the Emperor Penguin
#41: Moonlight on the Magic Flute

Magic Tree House® Fact Trackers

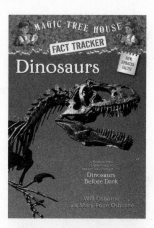

Dinosaurs
Knights and Castles
Mummies and Pyramids
Pirates
Rain Forests
Space
Titanic
Twisters and Other Terrible Storms
Dolphins and Sharks
Ancient Greece and the Olympics
American Revolution
Sabertooths and the Ice Age
Pilgrims
Ancient Rome and Pompeii
Tsunamis and Other Natural Disasters
Polar Bears and the Arctic
Sea Monsters
Penguins and Antarctica
Leonardo da Vinci
Ghosts
Leprechauns and Irish Folklore
Rags and Riches: Kids in the Time of Charles Dickens
Snakes and Other Reptiles
Dog Heroes
Abraham Lincoln
Pandas and Other Endangered Species
Horse Heroes
Heroes for All Times
Soccer
Ninjas and Samurai
China: Land of the Emperor's Great Wall
Sharks and Other Predators

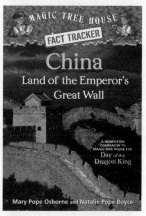

More Magic Tree House®

Games and Puzzles from the Tree House
Magic Tricks from the Tree House
My Magic Tree House Journal
Magic Tree House Survival Guide
Animal Games and Puzzles

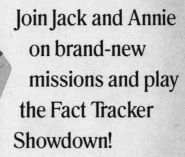
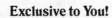